Origins

A Matter of Life and Death

Mick Gowar

Contents

OXFORD
UNIVERSITY PRESS

Introduction

This book is about adventure and danger. It's also about life and death decisions. You will read about people who never gave up, even when everything looked hopeless.

Captain William Bligh, HMS *Bounty*

Captain Bligh's best friend, Fletcher Christian, stole his ship and put him to sea in an open boat. With only the sun and stars to guide him, Bligh **navigated** across more than 4800 kilometres of ocean – and saved the lives of eighteen shipmates, too.

Alexander Selkirk

Alexander Selkirk lived alone on a desert island for more than four years. He had to make everything (his house, his clothes) using only a few simple tools he'd brought with him.

Ernest Shackleton

Ernest Shackleton was a **polar explorer**. On one of his polar trips his ship was crushed by ice but he didn't give up. For two years he led his men across the ice and sea to safety.

You will also find in this book:

- information on navigating using only the sun and an ordinary wristwatch

  See pages 8–9

- a quiz – see how good you'd be at making life or death decisions

  See pages 14–15

- a brand new game called *The Worst Journey In The World* to try out.

  See pages 25–29

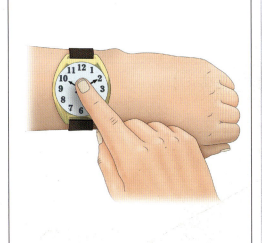

William Bligh, castaway

Mutiny on the *Bounty*

Mutiny is when sailors, soldiers or pilots refuse to obey the orders of their officers and take control of a ship, fort or airfield themselves. Punishments for mutiny can be severe.

HMS *Bounty*

In 1789 HMS *Bounty* was on a **mission** to take breadfruit plants from the island of Tahiti, in the Pacific Ocean, right across the world to the West Indies. The ship's captain was William Bligh and his second in command was Fletcher Christian. Bligh and Christian were old friends.

Tahiti was a beautiful island paradise. *Bounty* stayed there for many months.

When the time came to set sail for the West Indies, the sailors didn't want to leave Tahiti. Captain Bligh ordered the ship to sail but the men were very angry. After a few days at sea they mutinied.

The mutiny on the *Bounty*

Just before sunrise Mr Christian and the Master At Arms came into my cabin while I was fast asleep, and **seizing** me tied my hands with a cord and threatened instant death if I made the least noise. Mr Christian had a **cutlass** and the others were armed with **muskets** and **bayonets**. I was now carried on deck in my shirt, with my wrists tied behind my back, where I found no man to rescue me.

Extract from *William Bligh's log*, April 1789

Eighteen members of the crew refused to join the mutiny. They and Bligh were put in the ship's boat, which was less than 9 metres long and 2 metres wide. Bligh begged for a sextant and his papers and charts. Bligh and his men were also given five days' supply of food and water.

The mutineers put Bligh and his men on the ship's boat.

At first Bligh and his men landed on the nearby island of Tofua but they were chased off by the natives.

Bligh's decision

The nearest islands where they might have been welcome were Tahiti but Bligh was sure the mutineers would sail back to Tahiti. Bligh decided to sail to the island of Timor, thousands of kilometres away.

This is a sextant. It's an **instrument** which sailors use to help them work out where they are. By looking through the little telescope, you can compare where a boat is to the position of the sun or stars.

Bligh's journey

PACIFIC OCEAN

N

Java

Timor

Tofua

Tahiti

New Holland (Australia)

Bligh was a superb navigator. In 47 days he steered the tiny boat 5823 kilometres from Tofua to Timor, using just his sextant and charts.

Occasionally Bligh and his men stopped at small, **uninhabited** islands to gather shellfish, like oysters and clams, to eat. They also collected fresh water from springs. Food was scarce. By the time they arrived in Timor, they looked like walking skeletons.

Our bodies were nothing but skin and bones, our limbs were full of sores and we were clothed in rags: in this condition, with the tears of joy and gratitude flowing down our cheeks, the people of Timor beheld us with a mixture of horror, surprise and pity.

Extract from William Bligh's book, *A Voyage To The South Sea*

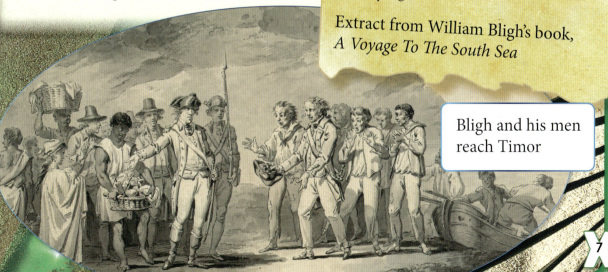

Bligh and his men reach Timor

7

Navigating with a compass

One of the most important instruments to help you find your way is a compass. A compass has a floating **magnetic** needle. A compass needle always points to the north. When you know which way is north, you can then, with the help of a map, work out which way you have to go.

A compass

Here's a very useful way for finding your way using the sun – just like William Bligh did. You don't need a sextant, all you need is:

- an ordinary wristwatch
- a small twig or grass stem.

How to turn a watch into a compass

1

Point the hour hand of your watch in the direction of the sun. Be careful to keep the watch very still. Do not look directly at the sun.

2

Count the numbers or marks between the hour hand and the number 12 on the watch's face.

3

Find the number or mark half-way between the hour hand and the number 12.

4

Place a twig on the half-way mark and across the watch.

5

The half-way point between the hour hand and the number 12 is south.

Can you use your watch to work out where these directions are?
- South
- North
- West
- East

Alexander Selkirk, stranded

Alexander Selkirk

The Juan Fernandez Islands are a tiny group of islands in the Pacific Ocean, about 600 kilometres off the coast of Chile. On 2 February, 1709, a British ship called *Duke* stopped at the Juan Fernandez Islands. On one of the islands the sailors found a Scottish seaman called Alexander Selkirk. He had been living alone on the island for four years.

Juan Fernandez Islands

PACIFIC OCEAN

C H I L E

N

The sailors find Selkirk

The boat went ashore and found Alexander Selkirk who had been on the island four years and four months, living on goats, cabbages that grow on trees, turnips and parsnips. He was clothed in goatskin breeches and cap, sewn together with thongs.

Edward Cooke, officer on board the *Duke*

Selkirk was the son of a Scottish shoemaker. He ran away to sea in 1697 and joined a **buccaneer** ship in the South Pacific.

By 1703, he was on a ship called *Cinque Ports*. It was a privateer, a kind of pirate ship, under the command of the British navy. Its job was to attack Spanish and French ships and steal their treasure.

A buccaneer ship

Selkirk was convinced that the ship was going to sink. He had a fierce argument with the ship's captain and demanded to be put ashore on the nearest island.

As soon as the ship's boat started to row away, Selkirk changed his mind. He called out to his shipmates to take him back to the ship, but they kept rowing.

Selkirk was alone on the island!

Before he left the ship, Selkirk chose the following things to take with him to help him survive on the island:

- an old-fashioned gun called a musket
- gunpowder and **ammunition** for his gun
- a **tinder** box to make fire with
- an axe
- a knife
- a kettle
- spare clothes
- bedding, including a roll of linen cloth
- enough food for two meals.

Like any **survival** expert, Selkirk was really clever at using his tools to make things from whatever he found around him.

To start with, Selkirk stayed on the seashore. He ate only fish and shellfish. He spent most of his time gazing out to sea, feeling sorry for himself.

Then Selkirk made his most important decision – he wasn't going to give up. He was going to make a new life for himself on the island.

He built two huts with pimento trees, covered them with long grass and lined them with the skins of wild goats. He made fire by rubbing two sticks of pimento wood together on his knee. In the smaller hut he kept his food and in the larger hut he slept.

When his clothes wore out, he made himself a cap of goatskin, which he stitched together with goatskin thongs he cut with his knife. He used a nail for a needle. He had a roll of linen cloth and sewed himself shirts with a nail and stitched them with wool he pulled out from his old stockings.

Captain Woodes-Rodgers, Captain of the *Duke*

Bear Grylls is a modern-day survival expert. You can read more about Bear Grylls on page 16.

Surviving like Selkirk

Selkirk made one very bad decision: to be put ashore. But before he left the ship he also made some good decisions. He chose some very useful tools to take with him. These tools helped him to survive on the island.

Here's a game you can play, either on your own or in a small group. Read the instructions very carefully.

 Could you make good decisions if you had to choose what you would need to survive?

Shipwreck

You are on a boat in the middle of the Atlantic Ocean. It's sinking!

You have to get into an open life raft. You can choose what you want to take with you in the life raft.

You can only take seven things from the list.
Which would you choose?

a shaving mirror

sextant

sea charts (maps of the ocean)

plastic sheeting

an FM radio receiver

a fishing line

fish hooks

a box of chocolate bars

nylon rope

a flare gun

six bottles of fresh water

a box of ten flares

If you're working in a group, you must all agree on your list. If you want to make the game even more difficult, give yourselves a time limit to come to an agreement – no more than ten minutes!

Turn over to the next page when you've made your choice.

Would you survive?

Former soldier Bear Grylls has written a book about survival.

Bear Grylls's Survival Principle

Protection, **Rescue**, **Water**, **Food**. This is the order of which is more important. You can last longer without food than you can without protection.

In 1998, at the age of 23, Bear Grylls was the youngest British person to climb Mount Everest. He is a best-selling author and presents a TV programme on surviving in the wilds.

These choices are based on Bear's PRWF principle.
Do you agree with them?

My choices

1   Plastic sheeting: to provide shelter and collect rainwater for drinking
2   Nylon rope: to tie down the sheeting and to tie you into the raft in bad weather
3   Six bottles of fresh water
4   Shaving mirror: to **signal** with, using the sun. The raft is in the middle of the ocean, so the best chance of surviving is to be rescued
5   Flare gun: for signalling
6   Box of ten flares: for signalling
7   Box of chocolate bars.

What I rejected

● Sextant and charts. Even if you could use them how would they help you? You are in the middle of the ocean in a life raft – that means you can't steer or power it.
● FM radio receiver. It's not a transmitter, so it couldn't be used to signal for help. It wouldn't even be good entertainment. You couldn't pick up any stations mid-ocean.
● Fishing line and hooks. You don't need as much skill or energy to unwrap a chocolate bar!

Ernest Shackleton, across the ice

Some people love to test themselves to the limit. Explorers, sailors and climbers show us how brave and resourceful people can be when faced with great dangers and great adventures.

In the early 1900s, explorers and sailors from Britain, Ireland, New Zealand and Norway were racing to be the first to reach the South Pole. One of those explorers was Ernest Shackleton.

Roald Amundsen, Norway

Ernest Shackleton, Ireland

Robert Falcon Scott, Great Britain

Frank Worsley, New Zealand

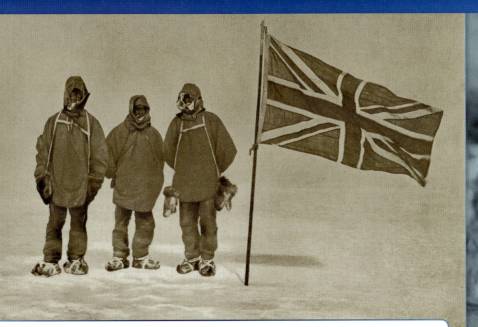

In 1908, Shackleton and his three men got within 156 kilometres of the South Pole but Shackleton decided to turn back. They were ill and running out of food. One of the men took this photo of Shackleton and his other two men just before they turned back.

In 1911, the Norwegian explorer Roald Amundsen won the race. He arrived at the South Pole 35 days ahead of a British explorer, Robert Falcon Scott.

Shackleton still wanted to go to the South Pole. He decided to organise the first expedition to walk across Antarctica from one side to the other. He bought a ship, *Endurance,* and set sail in 1914.

People wanted for hazardous journey

* Small wages
* Bitter cold
* Long months of complete darkness
* Constant danger
* Safe return doubtful
* Honour and recognition in case of success.

Apply to:
Ernest Shackleton

Trapped on the frozen sea

Endurance reached the islands of South Georgia in November 1914. Although this was the middle of the Antarctic summer, the weather was bitterly cold. By 5 December, instead of the explorers being on land, *Endurance* was trapped in ice in the Weddell Sea. Shackleton could have

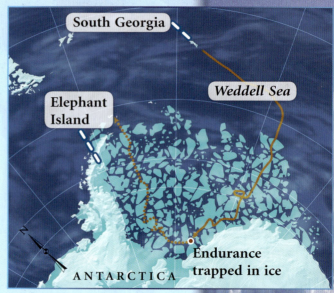

South Georgia

Elephant Island

Weddell Sea

Endurance trapped in ice

ANTARCTICA

turned back at this point but he decided to stay. Shackleton and the others camped on the ice and waited for the ice to melt.

Shackleton and his men even played football matches on the ice!

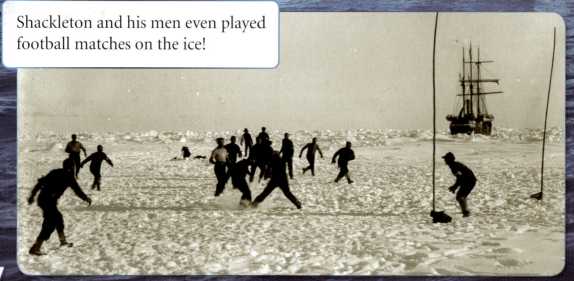

Then winter came. There was complete darkness for many days. The ice pressed down on the trapped ship. Shackleton and his men took everything they could off *Endurance*, including the lifeboats. They were just in time. *Endurance* was crushed by the ice and sank. Shackleton and his men were trapped on the frozen sea.

When the ice started to melt they got back into the lifeboats. Shackleton decided to row to Elephant Island, a tiny uninhabited island 100 kilometres away.

One of Shackleton's men took this photo of *Endurance* as it sank.

Shackleton encourages his men to pull the life boat across the ice.

The three lifeboats reached Elephant Island safely but two of the three boats were too badly damaged to sail any further. There were seals and penguins to eat but no ships stopped at Elephant Island. Somehow they had to get help. There was only one small lifeboat left.

Shackleton and his men landing on Elephant Island

Shackleton decided to leave most of the men on Elephant Island. He would sail with five of his men to the island of South Georgia, where there was a small village of fishermen, to get help. South Georgia was 1300 kilometres away!

Shackleton and five others set off in the lifeboat to get help.

The tiny boat sailed through terrible storms. The weather was freezing cold. They had to dodge huge icebergs. When they got close to South Georgia there were rocks to avoid, too. Eventually they landed safely but on the wrong side of the island.

Three of the men made camp. Shackleton and two others walked across the island. They had to climb a mountain range but eventually they reached the fishing village.

Four months after they'd set off, Shackleton and the others returned to Elephant Island with a rescue boat.

Despite the cold and poor food, everyone who sailed on *Endurance* survived.

The Worst Journey in the World!

Hi! My name is Chris Joyce, and I design computer games. I'm working on a new game based on Shackleton's voyage from Elephant Island to South Georgia.

The first thing I must decide is what sort of game it should be. As it is based on Shackleton's voyage, I think it should be an adventure game. Players will have to move a boat from Elephant Island to South Georgia. The boat will have to avoid **hazards**, such as icebergs and whales. If the boat hits the hazards, the player loses points. I'm going to try out a very simple version on paper – like a board game.

To try out the first version of the game for yourself you will need:

- a piece of squared paper
- a pen
- a pencil
- two players
- a dice.

On the next two pages, you will find the instructions.

The first version of the game

Rules of the game

Player 1 is Shackleton in his lifeboat. Player 1 is trying to get from Elephant Island to South Georgia.

Player 2 is trying to stop Player 1 reaching South Georgia.

1. Player 1 draws two islands on the squared paper. The island on the bottom left is Elephant Island and the one on the top right is South Georgia.

2. Player 2 draws eight rocks wherever they like between the islands.

3. Player 1 starts with 10 points. Every time they have a go they take 1 point from their score. If they hit a rock, they lose 1 point. If the score falls to 0, they lose. Player 1 moves 4 squares in each go, in any direction.

4. Player 2 throws the dice to decide the first square of Player 1's turn. The table below shows what each number means for Player 1.

Player 2 throws the dice a first time		
Number on the dice	What it means	What it means for Player 1
1	North wind	Move 1 square up
2	South wind	Move 1 square down
3	Hazard	
4	East wind	Move 1 square left
5	West wind	Move 1 square right
6	Hazard	

5. If the dice shows a 3 or a 6, Player 2 throws the dice again
    to decide which hazard Player 1 has to face.

Player 2 throws the dice a second time to decide the hazard		
Number on the dice	Hazard	What it means for Player 1
1	No wind	Take 1 from your score
2	Hit by killer whale	Take 1 from your score
3	Hit by wave	Take 1 from your score
4	Lost in fog	Move 2 squares west, take 1 from your score
5	Caught in a storm	Move 2 squares south, take 1 from your score
6	You hit an iceberg	Take 2 from your score

6. Player 1 then moves four squares, in any direction.
    They mark their route in pencil.

7. Player 2 throws the dice to decide the next square.
    And so on … .

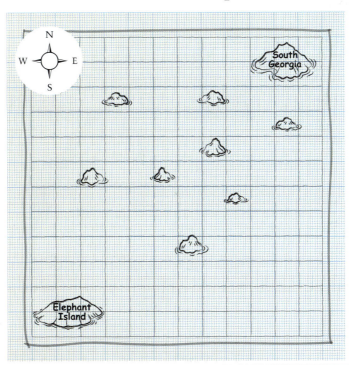

Redesigning the game

The next stage is to redesign the paper game for the computer.

I've decided that the computer version will be a one-player game. That means the computer will have to do everything Player 2 did in the paper version. To replace the dice, I have to make rules for the computer to follow. The computer will now decide the direction of the wind and when the boat might hit an iceberg or be attacked by a whale.

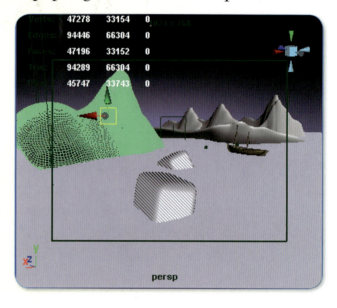

Now I have to start designing the game. I think it would be a great game for a hand-held console with two screens.

Two screens are ideal for this sort of game. The top screen could show the action of the game – the exciting pictures of the boat, the stormy seas and the leaping whale!

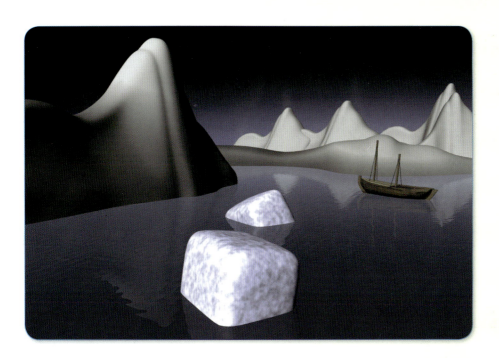

In the bottom screen, the player moves the boat across a squared map, like the paper version, using the stylus.

But will the player's journey be as difficult as Shackleton's was?

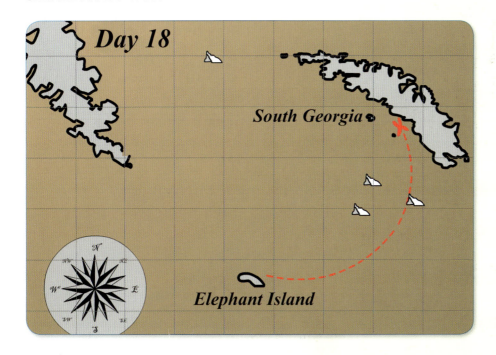

Day 18

South Georgia

Elephant Island

Glossary

ammunition	a supply of bullets to be fired from guns
bayonet	a long sharp knife that is fastened to the end of a rifle and used as a weapon
buccaneer	a sailor who attacked and robbed ships at sea
cutlass	a short sword with a curved blade that was used by pirates
explorer	a person who travels to unknown places in order to find out more about them
flare	something that produces a bright flame that is used as a signal
hazard	something that can be dangerous or cause damage
instrument	a tool or machine that you use for doing a job
magnetic	something that behaves like a magnet; that attracts objects made of iron towards it
mission	something that you feel is your duty to do
musket	an old kind of gun, with a long barrel
navigate	to make sure that a ship, plane or car is going in the right direction
polar	connected with the North or South Pole
seize	to grab something roughly
signal	a light, sound or movement that tells people what they should do, or that something is about to happen
survival	continuing to live, in spite of difficulty
tinder	dry material like wood or paper that can be used to light a fire
uninhabited	somewhere where no people are living

Index

To find out more about Dilemmas and Decisions read:

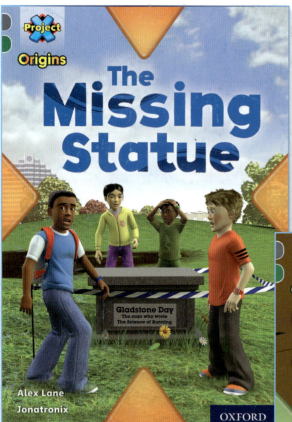

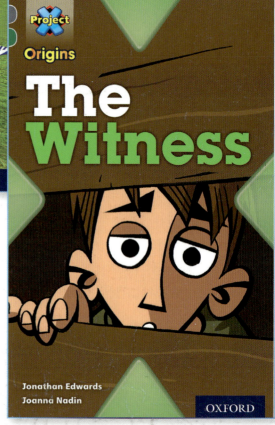